Super Simple Things to Do with Temperature

Fun and Easy Science for Kids

Kelly Doudna

Consulting Editor, Diane Craig, M.A./Reading Specialist

A Division of ABDO

ABDO
Publishing Company

To Adult Helpers

Learning about science is fun and simple to do. There are just a few things to remember to keep kids safe. Some activities in this book recommend adult supervision. Some use oily liquids, sharp objects, or stove burners. Be sure to review the activities before starting, and be ready to assist your budding scientist when necessary.

Key Symbols

In this book you will see some symbols. Here is what they mean.

 Hot. Get help! You will be working with something hot.

 Adult Help. Get help! You will need help from an adult.

 Sharp Object. Be careful! You will be working with a sharp object.

visit us at www.abdopublishing.com

Published by ABDO Publishing Company, a division of ABDO, P.O. Box 398166, Minneapolis, Minnesota 55439. Copyright © 2011 by Abdo Consulting Group, Inc. International copyrights reserved in all countries. No part of this book may be reproduced in any form without written permission from the publisher. Super SandCastle™ is a trademark and logo of ABDO Publishing Company.

Printed in the United States of America, North Mankato, Minnesota
102010
012011

 PRINTED ON RECYCLED PAPER

Editor: Liz Salzmann
Content Developer: Nancy Tuminelly
Cover and Interior Design and Production: Oona Gaarder-Juntti, Mighty Media, Inc.
Photo Credits: Kelly Doudna, Shutterstock
The following manufacturers/names appearing in this book are trademarks: McCormick®, Pyrex®, Salon Series™, Wesson®

Library of Congress Cataloging-in-Publication Data
Doudna, Kelly, 1963-
  Super simple things to do with temperature : fun and easy science for kids / Kelly Doudna.
    p. cm. -- (Super simple science)
  ISBN 978-1-61714-676-3
  1. Temperature--Experiments--Juvenile literature. 2. Science--Experiments--Juvenile literature.
I. Title.
  QC271.4.D684 2011
  536'.5078--dc22
                          2010020862

Super SandCastle™ books are created by a team of professional educators, reading specialists, and content developers around five essential components—phonemic awareness, phonics, vocabulary, text comprehension, and fluency—to assist young readers as they develop reading skills and strategies and increase their general knowledge. All books are written, reviewed, and leveled for guided reading, early reading intervention, and Accelerated Reader® programs for use in shared, guided, and independent reading and writing activities to support a balanced approach to literacy instruction.

Contents

Super Simple Science

Want to be a scientist? You can do it. It's super simple! Science is in things all around your house. Science is in a sock and in aluminum foil. Science is in a rubber band and in vegetable oil. Science is even in water and in food coloring. Science is everywhere. Try the **activities** in this book. You will find science right at home!

Temperature

Learning about science using **temperature** is super simple! Science explains what happens when you heat something up. Science explains why different things happen when you cool something down. In this book, you will see how temperature can help you learn about science.

Work Like a Scientist

Scientists have a special way of working. It is a series of steps called the Scientific Method. Follow the steps to work like a scientist.

1. Look at something. Watch it. What do you see? What does it do?

2. Think of a question about the thing you are watching. What is it like? Why is it like that? How did it get that way?

3. Try to answer your question.

4. Do a test to find out if you are right. Write down what happened.

5. Think about it. Were you right? Why or why not?

Keep Track

Want to be just like a scientist? Scientists keep notes about everything they do. So, get a notebook. When you do an experiment, write down what happens in each step. It's super simple!

Materials

index card

rubber bands

large paper clip

wool sock

timer

plastic wrap

baking pan

paper napkin

scissors

food coloring

aluminum foil

measuring cup

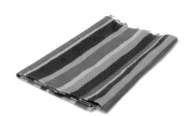
cotton cloth

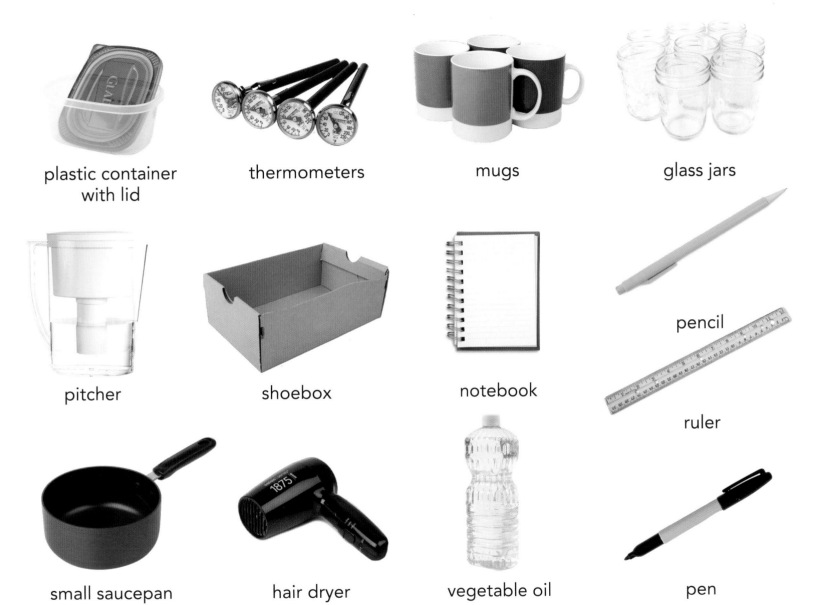

plastic container
with lid

thermometers

mugs

glass jars

pitcher

shoebox

notebook

pencil

ruler

small saucepan

hair dryer

vegetable oil

pen

7

Hot and Cold

What effect does temperature have on water?

Heating makes the water turn into steam.

Freezing causes water to **expand**.

8

Part 1: Hot

1 Measure ½ cup (118 ml) of water. Pour it into the saucepan. Place the pan on the stove.

2 Have your adult helper heat the water until it boils. You will know it is boiling when it bubbles.

3 Watch the water closely for a few minutes. Be careful not to get your face in the steam. What do you observe?

What's Going On?

When water boils, it turns into steam. Steam is a gas. The steam rises into the air. Don't let it boil too long. After a while all of the water will be gone!

9

Part 2: Cold

1 Fill the plastic container with water. Lay the cover over the top, but don't seal it.

2 Put the container in the freezer. Leave it there overnight.

3 Remove the container from the freezer. How does it look?

What's Going On?

Water **expands** when it freezes. The ice becomes bigger than the container. It pushes the cover up. If you let the ice thaw, the water will fit in the container again.

Insulation Fascination

How can you keep your hots hotter and your colds colder?

Some **materials** are better than others at keeping the **temperature** from changing.

Part 1

1 Line up the mugs. Have an adult help with the next step. Pour the same amount of very hot water into each mug. Be careful not to splash hot water on yourself.

2 Cover one mug each with the sock, cotton cloth, foil, and paper napkin. Use rubber bands to hold the covers in place.

3 Wait 45 minutes.

4 Take the covers off the mugs.

5 Put a **thermometer** in each mug. Which one is still the warmest?

Part 2

1 This time, pour cold water into each mug.

2 Cover one mug each with the sock, cotton cloth, foil, and paper napkin. Use rubber bands to hold the covers in place.

3 Wait 45 minutes.

4 Take the covers off the mugs.

5 Put a **thermometer** in each mug. Which one is still the coldest? Did the same **material** work the best for both hot and cold?

What's Going On?

Some things are good at holding in the heat or cold. Some things are not. What the material is made of makes a difference. The thickness of the material is also important.

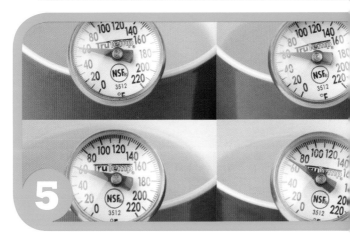

Heat by the Numbers

Why do animals and insects huddle together to stay warm?

A single jar cools off faster than a group of jars.

Part 1

1 Have your adult helper heat the water on the stove. When it begins to steam, have your helper fill one jar.

2 Cover the jar with plastic wrap. Poke a **thermometer** through the plastic wrap.

3 Wait for the **temperature** to stop rising. Record the temperature.

4 Wait 30 minutes. Record the temperature again.

5 Empty the jar.

Part 2

1 Group four jars so that they touch.

2 Have your adult helper reheat the water. When it begins to steam, have your helper fill all four jars.

3 Cover the jars with plastic wrap. Poke the **thermometers** through the plastic wrap. Make sure the jars are still touching.

4 Wait for the **temperatures** to be about the same as the first temperature in Part 1. Start the timer.

5 Wait 30 minutes. Record the temperatures. Are they higher or lower than in Part 1?

6 Wait until the temperatures are about the same as the second temperature in Part 1. How long did it take?

What's Going On?

The single jar loses heat from all sides. So it cools faster than the jars in a group. The grouped jars only lose heat from the outsides. So they cool more slowly.

Stretch It Out

How does temperature affect the stretch of a rubber band?

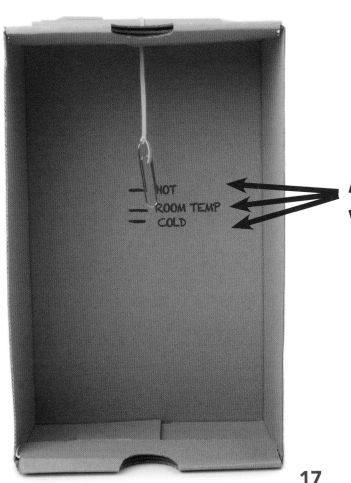

HOT
ROOM TEMP
COLD

A rubber band changes length when it is heated or cooled.

17

1 Cut the rubber band once. Tie one end around the pencil.

2 Stand the shoebox on a short side. Poke a hole in the top of the shoebox. Thread the loose end of the rubber band through it. Rest the pencil on the outside of the box.

3 Tie the loose end of the rubber band around the paper clip. Let the paper clip hang for a few minutes. If it touches the bottom, use a shorter rubber band.

4 On the inside of the box, mark how far down it hangs.

5 Put the shoebox in the refrigerator. After 20 minutes, open the door. Mark how far down the paper clip hangs after cooling. Then take the box out of the refrigerator.

6 Use the hair dryer to heat the rubber band for 5 minutes. Mark how far down the paper clip hangs after heating.

7 Compare all of the marks. Are you surprised by the results?

What's Going On?

Most **substances** get larger when they are heated. And they get smaller when they are cooled. A rubber band does the opposite. It gets longer when you cool it. It gets shorter when you heat it.

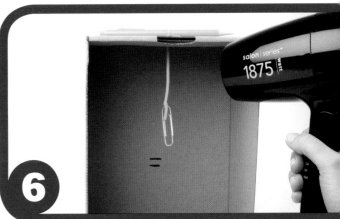

Purple Passion

Everyone knows that blue and red make purple, right?

What You'll Need
- 2 identical small jars
- measuring cup
- cold water
- food coloring
- hot water
- baking pan
- index card

Hot and cold water don't mix.

1. Place one jar in the baking pan. Fill it part way with very cold water. Stir in one drop of blue food coloring. Add more cold water until the jar is **completely** full.

2. Pour very hot water into the other jar. Stir in one drop of red food coloring. Add more hot water until the jar is completely full.

3. Place the index card over the top of the red jar. Press it down gently.

4. Keep pressing the index card and quickly turn the jar over. The index card will hold the water in. Set the upside-down jar on top of the blue jar. Line up the jar rims.

5. Have a helper hold onto both jars. Carefully pull the index card out from between them. What happens?

What's Going On?

The cold and hot water don't mix. That's because cold water has a higher **density** than hot water. It stays on the bottom. Hot water has a lower density than cold water. It stays on the top.

Top and Bottom

Oil floats on water, right?

The ice cube floats in oil.

The oil floats on water.

22

1. Fill the jar half full with vegetable oil.

2. Pour some water into the jar. What happens?

3. Now add the ice cube. What happens this time?

What's Going On?

Oil has a lower **density** than liquid water. So it floats on top of the water. But when water freezes into ice, it **expands** and its density increases. So the ice cube floats in the oil.

Conclusion

Congratulations! You found out that science can be super simple! And, you learned about **temperature**. Keep your thinking cap on. How else can you experiment using temperature?

Glossary

activity – something you do for fun or to learn about something.

completely – entirely or in every way.

congratulations – something you say to someone who has done well or accomplished something.

density – how heavy something is for its size.

expand – to become larger.

material – something that other things can be made of, such as fabric, plastic, or metal.

substance – anything that takes up space, such as a solid object or a liquid.

temperature – a measure of how hot or cold something is.

thermometer – a tool used to measure temperature.